USBORNE FIRST NATURE

ANIMALS BIRDS & FISHES

WILD ANIMALS

A Wood Mouse is hidden near this Leopard. Can you find 15 more Wood Mice hidden in this section of the book?

Looking at mammals

Mammals are different from all the other animals in the world. They are the only animals that have fur or hair. Female mammals are the only animals that produce milk to feed to their young. You are a mammal.

Fallow Deer feeding her fawn.

All mammals breathe air, even mammals that live in water.

A mammal has a good brain.

A mammal makes the inside of its body stay at about the same temperature — even when it is hot or cold outside.

All mammals have some fur or hair on their body.

▲
Musk Oxen have lots of hair. This keeps them warm.

Porcupines have special hairs, called quills.

Elephants ▶ have only a few hairs.

Many mammals have two kinds of hair in their coat. Beavers have a thick layer of short, soft hairs under a layer of long, rough hairs. Only the long hairs get wet in water.

Bactrian Camel

Some mammals, such as Camels, grow two new coats every year. This Camel is growing its thin summer coat. Its thick winter coat falls out so fast that the hairs come off in large chunks.

winter coat

summer coat

3

Legs and feet

Most mammals move around on four legs.

ankle

Pandas walk on their whole foot.

ankle

Foxes walk on their toes.

ankle

Deer walk on their toe nails.

Back feet land in front of front feet.

Otters use their tail to change direction.

Mountain Hares have feet like snowshoes. Their feet are wide and flat and have lots of fur underneath. This helps them to walk or run over the snow without sinking in very far.

Otters have skin between their toes. They use their feet like flippers to push them through the water.

4

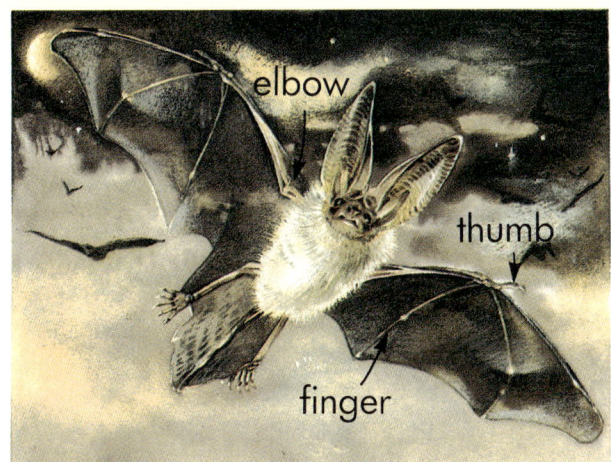

elbow

thumb

finger

The only mammals that can fly are bats. They use their arms as wings. Each wing is made of skin. The skin is stretched over the bones of the arms and fingers.

Kangaroo Rats hop around on two legs. They use their long back legs to make huge leaps. Their tail helps them to balance.

Long, thin toes for holding on to branches.

Spider Monkeys use their strong tail like an extra arm or leg. They curl the tip of the tail around branches to help them swing through the trees.

5

Teeth and feeding

Many mammals feed mainly on plants. They have a lot of grinding teeth because plants are hard to chew.

Chipmunks carry food in cheek pouches.

Horny pad is under here.

The front teeth of a Chipmunk never stop growing. Its teeth do not get too long as it wears them down when it feeds.

Bighorn Sheep have no front teeth in their top jaw. Instead they have a horny pad to bite off the tops of plants.

Long tongue pulls leaves off branches.

Giraffe

Eland

Zebra

Dik-dik

Many different mammals can feed close together on the African grasslands. This is because they eat different kinds of plants and feed at different heights. You can see this if you look carefully at the mammals in the picture above.

fruit

Dead
Vole

Long, sensitive
fingers help
to find and
catch food.

fish

Koalas feed only on the leaves of Gum Trees. They will die if they cannot find the right sort of Gum Tree to feed on.

Racoons feed on plants and animals. They eat living things and dead things. They can usually find enough to eat.

Long, pointed teeth to grip an animal's throat and strangle it.

Cheetah

Gazelle

Razor-sharp cheek teeth to tear meat.

Some mammals feed mainly on other animals. They use up a lot of energy catching their food. Cheetahs may be too tired to eat for up to 15 minutes after they have killed an animal. But meat is very nourishing, so they do not feed every day.

7

Mammals at night

More than half the mammals in the world come out at night.

Pupil opens wide to let in lots of light.

Sticky pads on toes help to grip branches.

The Tarsier has huge eyes and special ears that help it to see and hear well at night. It leaps through the trees and pounces on insects and small animals.

Potto

Many mammals have a special layer at the back of their eyes. This layer helps them to see in the dark. It makes their eyes glow if a light shines on them.

Badgers use their sharp sense of smell and good hearing to move around and feed at night. They find food by sniffing the ground with their sensitive noses.

fold of skin

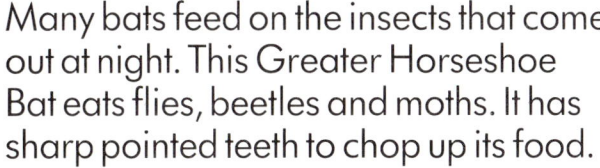

Many bats feed on the insects that come out at night. This Greater Horseshoe Bat eats flies, beetles and moths. It has sharp pointed teeth to chop up its food.

Sugar Gliders feed on flowers and insects at night. They stretch open the folds of skin along the sides of their bodies to glide quietly from tree to tree.

The Red Fox hunts at night. When it hears and smells a mouse in the grass, the Fox leaps up in the air like this. It will land with its front paws on the mouse.

Escaping from enemies

sharp
scales →

Squirrels escape from enemies by climbing trees. They are small and light and can leap on to very thin branches. Most of their enemies cannot follow.

Pangolins have horny scales like a suit of armour. The back edge of each scale is sharp. When they roll into a tight ball, their enemies cannot hurt them.

1. This Spiny Anteater has sharp spines on its back. It burrows into the ground to escape enemies.

2. It digs straight down with its long claws and sinks out of sight in about one minute.

3. When it is buried, its enemies leave it alone. The spines may cut them if they try to dig it up.

Skunk holds tail up to say "Go away or I will squirt you with smelly liquid".

summer

winter

Skunks squirt a nasty liquid at enemies. The liquid comes from a gland under the tail. Most enemies leave them alone.

The Mountain Hare lives in places where it snows in winter. It has a white coat in winter and a brown coat in summer. This helps it to hide from enemies, such as Foxes.

Many mammals that live in forests or jungles have stripes or spots on their fur. They match the colours and patterns on the trees and bushes. This helps them to hide from their enemies. There are eight mammals in this African jungle. Can you find them all?

11

Homes

Mammals build homes to keep them warm, dry and safe from enemies.

Rabbits live in a maze of tunnels, which they dig under the ground. Their home is called a warren. They run into the warren to escape from enemies.

The female Harvest Mouse builds a home for her young. She tears grass leaves into strips and weaves them into a round nest. It is warm and dry inside.

The cubs are born in the middle of winter.

The female Polar Bear digs a cave of ice and snow to spend the winter in. She does not come out until the weather gets warmer in spring.

molehill

The only home Chimpanzees make is a nest to sleep in. They build the nest near the top of a tree. They bend branches over to make a cushion of leaves.

A Mole spends most of its life inside its home. It uses its front feet like shovels to dig out tunnels in the soil. It feeds and sleeps in these tunnels.

air hole   The home is called a lodge.

This is what a Beaver's home looks like inside. The young are safe from enemies.

underwater entrances

Finding a mate

female

male

Siberian Tiger

male

female

Female mammals often give off a special smell when they are ready to mate. A male Harvest Mouse sniffs a female to see if she is ready to mate.

Tigers play together before they mate. This female is asking the male to mate with her. She bites him gently and then rubs her body against his.

females

The antlers fall off when the mating season ends.

Once a year, a male Red Deer rounds up a group of females for mating. He roars loudly to tell other males how strong he is. If another male roars as often as he does, they fight with their antlers. The strongest male wins the females.

Male antelopes, such as this Uganda Kob, have to dance in front of a female before they mate with her.

male   female   male   female

1. The male Kob holds his head up to show off the white patch under his chin. He stretches out his front legs to show off his black stripes.

2. Then he holds his front leg out very stiff and straight. He taps the female's side gently. If she stands still, he will mate with her.

Male and female Red Foxes dance together before they mate. They stand on their back legs and hug each other with their front legs. They hold their mouths open and make a chattering call.

Eggs and birth

After a female mammal has mated, a baby may start to grow inside her. Most baby mammals stay inside their mother until they have grown all the parts of their bodies. Then they are ready to be born.

When Zebras are born, they can see, hear and smell and have hair all over their bodies. They can run about an hour after they are born. They stay close to the other Zebras. This helps to keep them safe from enemies.

birth sac

When Dormice are born, they are helpless. They are blind and deaf and have no hair on their bodies. They are born in a nest, which helps to keep them warm and safe from enemies.

A few mammals are born before they grow all the parts of their bodies. Most of them finish developing in a pouch on their mother's body.

pouch

Close-up of the birth opening. The baby climbs upwards.

As soon as a baby Kangaroo is born, it has to crawl from the birth opening up to its mother's pouch. This takes about three minutes. The baby is so small, it would fit into a teaspoon.

Looking inside the pouch

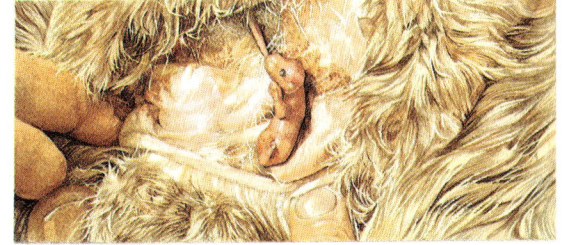

The baby holds on to a teat and sucks milk from its mother. It stays in the pouch for six months. By then, it has grown all the parts of its body.

The Platypus and the Spiny Anteaters are unusual mammals that lay eggs. A baby grows inside each egg.

The Platypus lays her eggs in a nest of leaves and grass. The eggs have a soft shell.

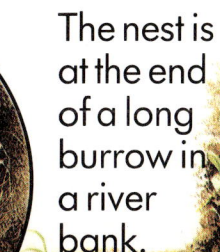

The nest is at the end of a long burrow in a river bank.

17

Growing up

Japanese Macaque

The baby stays with its mother for two or three years.

White-tailed Deer

Most mammals spend a lot of time licking their young. This keeps them clean and healthy. It also forms a bond between mother and young.

A baby mammal sucks milk from glands on its mother's body. The glands produce milk as soon as a baby is born. The milk is rich in foods the baby needs.

A Tigress picks up her cubs in her mouth to carry them to a safe place. The cubs do not get hurt as they keep still and their mother's jaws do not shut properly.

African Elephant

Mountain Goats play games with their mother and the other young goats. This helps them to learn how to balance and climb on the steep mountain slopes.

This mother Elephant is protecting her calf from an enemy. The young Elephant is too small to look after itself. It stays close to its mother.

White-toothed Shrews go out with their mother when they are about a week old. They hold on to each other in a long line so they do not get lost.

Living in a group

Lions live in a group called a pride. The female Lions are called Lionesses. They do most of the hunting. They also feed the cubs and look after them. The male Lions keep a safe area for the pride to live in.

An adult male has a thick mane. This protects his head and neck in fights. It also helps him to attract a female.

Lionesses hunt in teams. They are more likely to catch large animals if they hunt together.

This is a young male. He will leave the pride when he is about three years old.

The cubs spend a lot of time playing. This helps them learn how to fight and hunt.

A Lioness usually stays in the pride for life. She may feed any of the cubs. This helps them survive.

Chimpanzees live in a group called a community. The males defend the group from enemies. They often travel and feed with other males. Females look after the young.

A Chimpanzee may share its food with other Chimps in the group. One Chimp may stare at another to ask for food.

There is a top male in each group. He often charges about like this making a lot of noise. This shows the other Chimps he is in charge.

Chimps crouch down like this when they meet a more important Chimp. This Chimp may pat them to say "I will not attack you".

Woodland Chimps catch Termites by poking a grass stem into their nest. Young Chimps watch their parents to find out how to do this.

Chimpanzees spend a lot of time grooming their fur. This helps to keep them clean and healthy. Grooming also calms the Chimps and helps them to stay good friends.

Sea Mammals

The only mammals that spend their whole lives in the sea are Dolphins, Whales and Sea Cows. They have few hairs and no back legs.

A Dolphin comes to the surface to breathe air through its blowhole.

A Dolphin's body is a good shape for moving fast through the water. It moves its strong tail up and down to push it along. It uses its flippers and the fin on its back to change direction.

A Dolphin's teeth are all the same. They are good for catching fish.

Mouth of a Humpback Whale.

bony plates

Manatees are a kind of Sea Cow.

Some Whales have no teeth. Instead they have rows of bony plates, which end in a thick, hairy fringe. The fringe strains tiny animals from the sea water.

This Manatee calf is sucking milk from a teat near its mother's flipper. Manatees are born in the water and can swim as soon as they are born.

Seals, Sea Lions and Walruses spend only part of their lives in the sea. They have back legs and most of them have a coat of short hair.

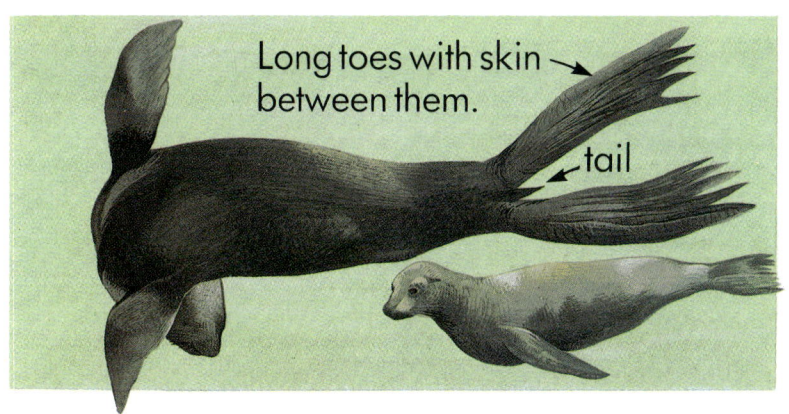

Long toes with skin between them.

tail

A Sea Lion's smooth, thin body helps it to swim fast underwater. It uses its front flippers to push it along. It uses its back flippers to change direction. It has only a short tail.

Walruses use their long teeth to dig up shellfish from the sea floor. They also use their teeth for fighting.

Pups grow fast on their mother's rich milk.

A layer of skin comes off with the old fur coat.

Seals, Sea Lions and Walruses come out of the sea every year to give birth, mate and grow a new coat of fur.
This is a group of Elephant Seals. The males fight each other to win their own area on the beach. They will mate with all the females in their area.

Picture puzzle

The Rabbit has to get back to his home on the other side of the maze. Can you help him to find the right path? Part of the maze goes through the Giraffe's body. Can you name all the mammals in the maze?

START →

HOME

BIRDS

Games in this book

2. Watch the bird fly

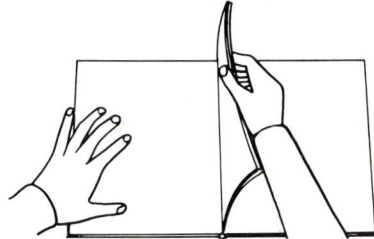

Hold the Bird pages like this.

1. Hunt the Grasshopper

Some birds eat Grasshoppers. Can you find 13 more Grasshoppers in the Bird pages?

Watch the top right hand corner and flick the pages over fast.

watch here

Looking at birds

A bird is like
an aeroplane.

Its shape helps it to
move fast through the air.

A bird is like
a bat.

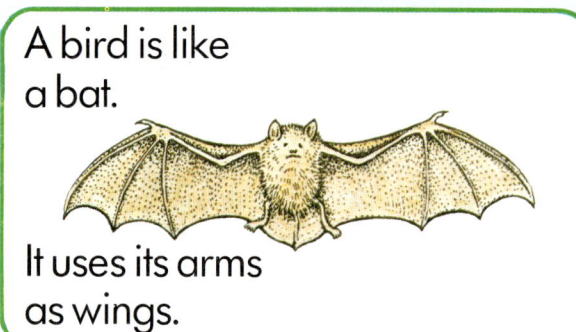

It uses its arms
as wings.

Swallow

A bird is like
a weightlifter.
It has strong arm
and chest muscles.

A bird is like
a balloon.
It has lots of air
inside its body.

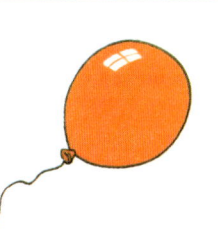

Birds are the only
animals in the world
that have feathers.

Birds have three kinds of feathers.

1. Down feathers.
They help keep the bird warm.

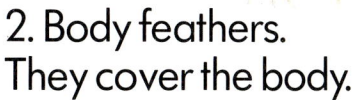

2. Body feathers.
They cover the body.

3. Flight feathers.
They help the bird to fly.

Greylag goose

Down feathers are under the body feathers.

body feathers

flight feathers

Birds grow a new set of feathers every year.

A goose cannot fly while its new flight feathers are growing.

baby goose

down feathers

Baby birds have down feathers to help keep them warm.

Bee-eater

Hummingbird

Wood Warbler

Taking off and flying

Blue Tit

When birds want to take off, they leap into the air and flap their wings as fast as they can.

Mute Swan

Some birds are too heavy to leap into the air. Before they can take off they have to run along flapping their wings.

Mallard

Tawny Owl

Golden Eagle

Eagles stretch out their wide wings and float on the air.

Large birds, like eagles, flap their wings slowly. Small birds flap their wings very fast.

A wing is like an arm. It bends in two places.

Common Tern

Birds twist or bend their wings to turn in the air. Look at the way the other birds on this page bend their wings.

Kingfisher

Galah

Albatross

Goldfinch

29

Why do birds fly?

To build their nests in high places.

To go to warmer places where there is more food.

To catch food in the air.

To look for food on the ground.

To escape from their enemies.

Why do birds land?

To feed or rest in trees.

To feed on the ground.

To drink.

To rest.

To feed their young.

To sit on their eggs.

To meet other birds and mate.

Legs and feet

Puffin

Birds walk on their toes.
They can run or hop
along the ground.

A bird's leg
bends here.

A bird puts out its feet to land.
It also spreads out its tail and
wings to slow down.

Marabou Stork

Starling

This bird rests on branches.
When it bends its legs,
its toes lock on to the branch.

Some birds rest on the ground.
Storks often sit like this when they rest.

Birds often stand on one leg. They tuck the other leg under their feathers to keep it warm.

Coot

Mallard

Water birds have skin between their toes. The skin helps them to use their feet as paddles and to walk on mud without sinking in.

Snowy Owl

The feathers on its feet help it to walk on the snow without sinking in.

The Snowy Owl has claws like daggers. It kills with its feet. Its feet are covered with feathers to keep them warm.

Beaks and feeding

Birds have no teeth so they cannot chew food. They swallow food whole and then grind it up in their stomachs.

Kookaburra

Magpie

Black Kite

This bird uses its hooked beak to tear up its food.

strainer

Shoveler

This duck uses its beak as a strainer. It collects tiny plants and animals from the top of the water.

Pelicans

pouch

Crossbill

A Pelican uses its huge beak to scoop fish from the water. Its beak can hold more food than its stomach.

Hummingbird

Rosella

Birds have different kinds of beaks because they eat different kinds of food. These seashore birds can feed close together because they eat different animals.

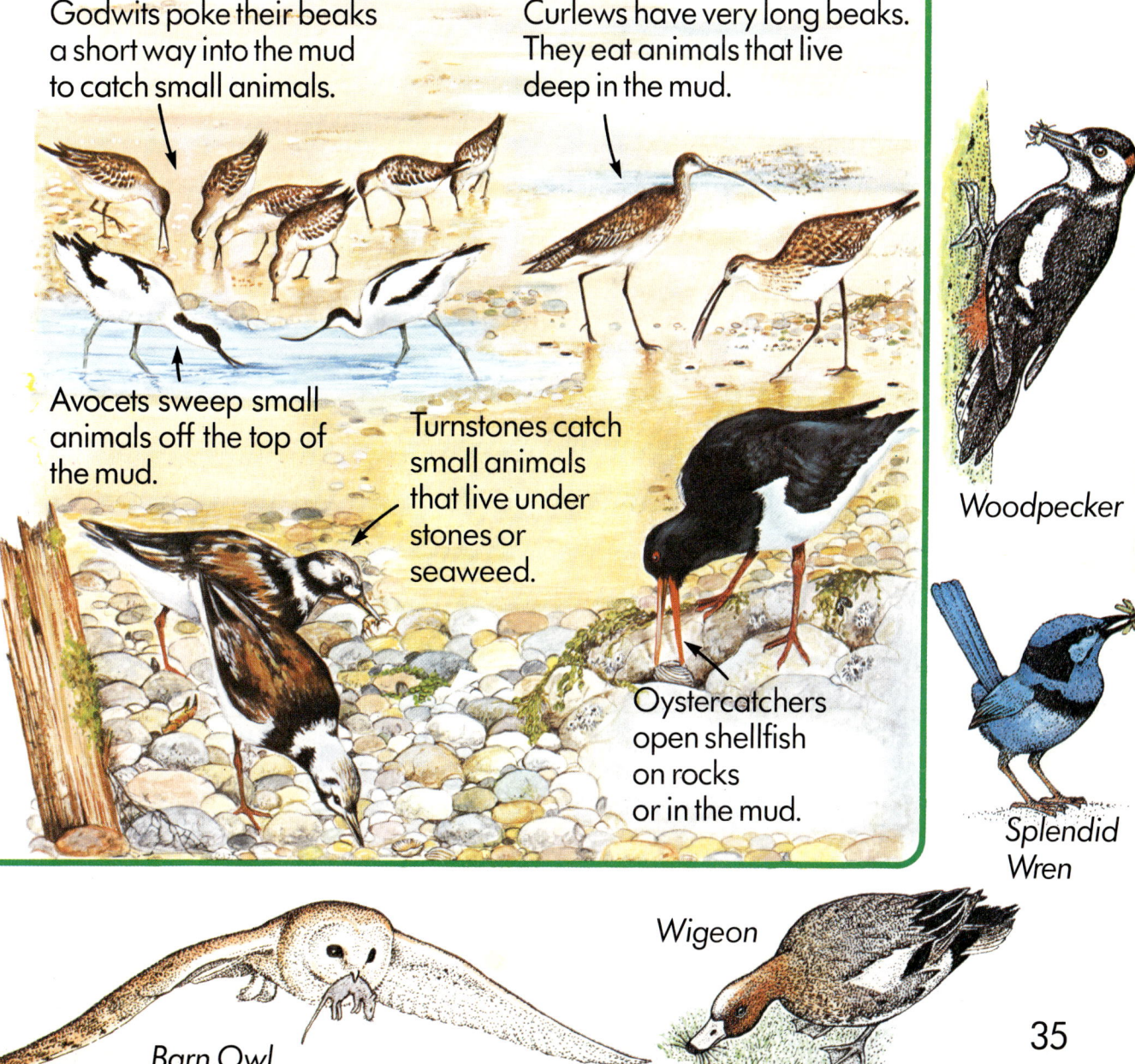

Godwits poke their beaks a short way into the mud to catch small animals.

Curlews have very long beaks. They eat animals that live deep in the mud.

Avocets sweep small animals off the top of the mud.

Turnstones catch small animals that live under stones or seaweed.

Oystercatchers open shellfish on rocks or in the mud.

Woodpecker

Splendid Wren

Wigeon

Barn Owl

Colours

Many birds match the colour of the leaves and branches of the trees they rest in. This helps them to hide from their enemies.

There are seven birds in this picture. Can you see them all?

Frogmouth

When birds are sitting on eggs, they need to be hidden. This female Nightjar is sitting on her eggs. She is hard to see.

The Australian Frogmouth sleeps all day in a tree. It sits very still with its head up. It looks just like a broken branch.

Birds may use their colours to recognize each other.

Oystercatchers live together in big groups. If some of the birds fly off
to a new feeding place, the others soon follow. They recognize each other
by their colours and the calls that they make.

female

males

Male and female Mallards are different colours. Male Mallards are most colourful
in the breeding season. They show off their bright colours in a special dance.
This attracts a female for mating.

Song and dance

Birds sing most of all in the breeding season.

Male Blackbirds sing to attract female Blackbirds.

female Blackbird

Male Blackbirds also sing to tell other male Blackbirds "This is where I live so keep away".

Tawny Owls

Owls find each other in the dark by calling.

The male Pigeon has to dance in front of the female before he can mate with her. He turns in circles and "coos" loudly all the time.

1. The male makes himself look big. He puffs out his neck feathers.

2. He spreads out his tail like a fan and bows to the female.

female

male

female

male

Peacock

Peahen

The peacock uses his long feathers in a dance to attract a female. The long feathers fall out when the breeding season is over.

Guillemot eggs

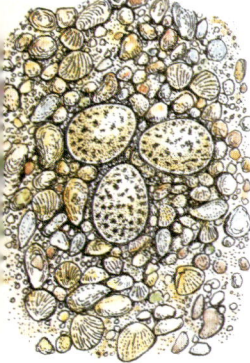

Oystercatcher eggs

Eggs and nests

Soon after a female bird has mated, she lays her eggs. If she kept all her eggs inside her until they were ready to hatch, she would probably be too heavy to fly.

The female Common Tern lays her eggs on the ground. A baby Tern grows inside each egg.

The eggs match the colour of the ground around them. It is hard for enemies to see them.

When baby Terns hatch, they are covered with down. The down helps keep them warm.

If an enemy is about, the baby Terns crouch down so they are difficult to see.

Rook eggs

Eider Duck eggs

Most birds build nests. The nest hides the eggs and baby birds from enemies. It helps to keep them warm. Birds also sit on their eggs to keep them warm. If the eggs get cold, the baby birds inside them will die.

Song Thrushes

Rock Warbler nest

The male Thrush feeds the female. She sits on the eggs for two weeks.

Baby birds that hatch in nests are naked and blind. Their parents look after them.

Golden Oriole eggs

Hummingbird eggs

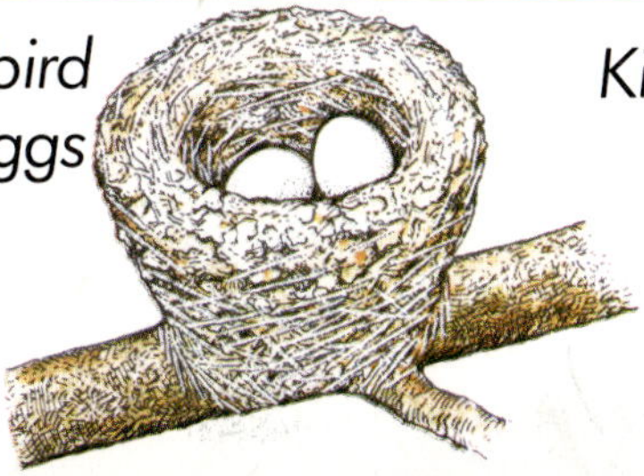

Kingfisher nest

Growing up

Song Thrush

Thrushes collect food from their home area near the nest.

Baby Thrushes stay in the nest for two weeks until most of their feathers have grown.

Baby birds are always hungry. When their parents land on the nest, the baby birds open their beaks wide and call loudly. The bright colours inside their beaks make their parents feed them.

Baby Herring Gulls peck the red spot to get a meal.

Older Herring Gulls peck at the top of the beak.

Herring Gulls may have to fly far away to collect food for their babies. They swallow the food that they collect. When they get back, they cough up the food for the babies to eat.

Baby geese may watch their parents to find out what to eat.

They may sit on their mother's back if they are cold or tired.

A short time after they hatch, baby geese can swim. They will go into the water to escape from enemies.

Young geese take about six weeks to grow all their feathers.
They can now fly, but they may practise twisting and turning in the air.
They may also practise taking off and landing.

43

Resting and preening

At night most birds find a safe place to rest. They do not like flying at night because they cannot see well in the dark.

Hundreds of Starlings often fly to the same place every evening. They all rest together for the night.

Some birds tuck their beaks under their wings when they sleep. They fluff out their feathers to keep themselves warm.

Sparrows

Lots of Wrens may sleep together to keep warm.

Birds don't fall out of trees when they sleep. This is because when they bend their legs, their toes lock on to the branch.

All birds clean and tidy up their feathers. This is called preening. Most birds also spread oil on their feathers to keep them in good condition.

Birds squeeze oil out of a gland just above the tail.

Herring Gulls

oil gland

Lovebirds

Some birds preen each other.

Song Thrush

Some birds have a bath.

45

Birds that do not fly

The Ostrich is the largest bird in the world. It is too heavy to fly and it has only small wing feathers. The Ostrich cannot fly away from enemies, but it can look after itself in other ways.

It is taller than a man. It can see enemies a long way away.

The beak of an Ostrich is strong enough to crack the skull of an enemy.

The Ostrich has long legs with strong muscles. It can run faster than its enemies.

On its big toe, it has a dangerous claw. It could kick an enemy to death.

big toe

Penguins do not fly with their wings. Do you know how they use them?

Penguins use their wings as flippers. They can swim very fast on top of the water or under the water.

Penguins use their wings to help them balance.

Penguins use their wings and their beaks when they quarrel.

These Penguins are hunting for fish.

Penguins can jump out of the sea.

Rockhopper Penguins

47

Picture puzzle

There are 13 birds hidden in this picture.
Can you find them all?

FISHES

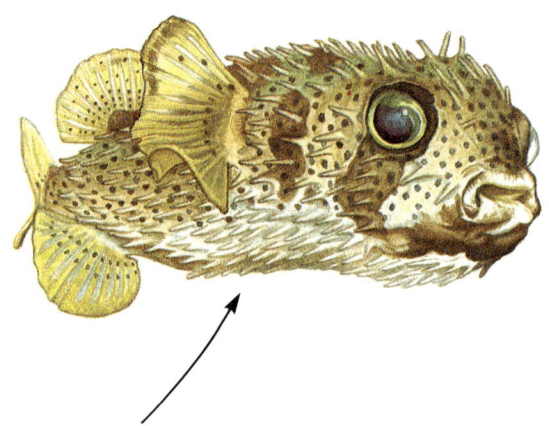

Porcupine Fishes normally
look like this.

When they are frightened, they
can blow themselves up with
water like this. Then other
fishes are less likely to eat them.

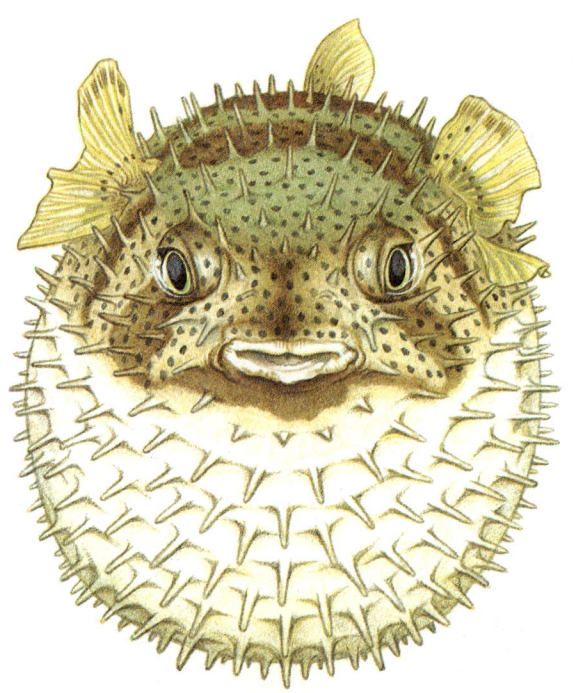

What is a fish?

Fishes are animals that live in water. They breathe through gills and have a skeleton inside the body. Their bodies usually stay at the same temperature as the water around them. Most fishes lay eggs.

The gills are under the gill cover.

Goldfish eggs

Goldfish

The skeleton supports the body and fins.

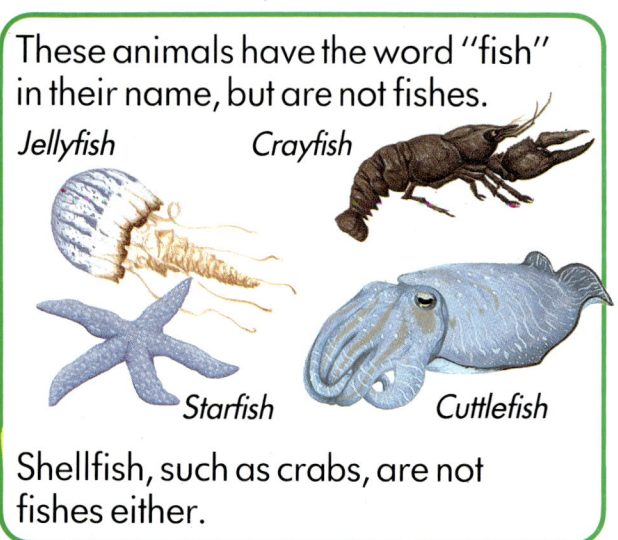

These animals have the word "fish" in their name, but are not fishes.

Jellyfish

Crayfish

Starfish

Cuttlefish

Shellfish, such as crabs, are not fishes either.

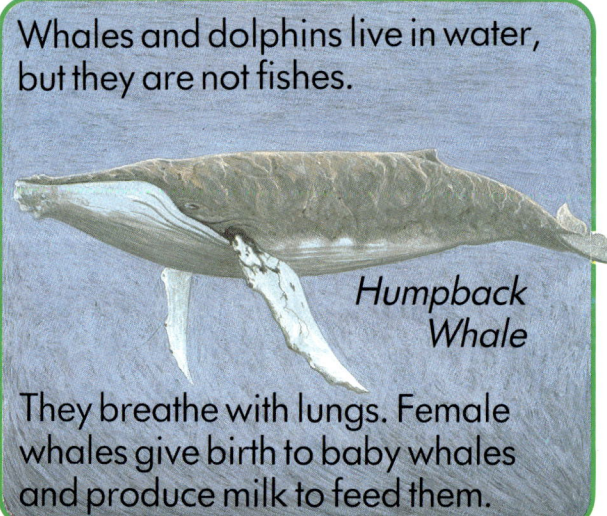

Whales and dolphins live in water, but they are not fishes.

Humpback Whale

They breathe with lungs. Female whales give birth to baby whales and produce milk to feed them.

There are three main kinds of fishes.

1. Bony fishes

Most fishes have a skeleton made of bone. Their bodies are usually covered by very thin scales.

Bony fishes have a gill cover.

Thin, overlapping scales.

Perch

2. Sharks and Rays

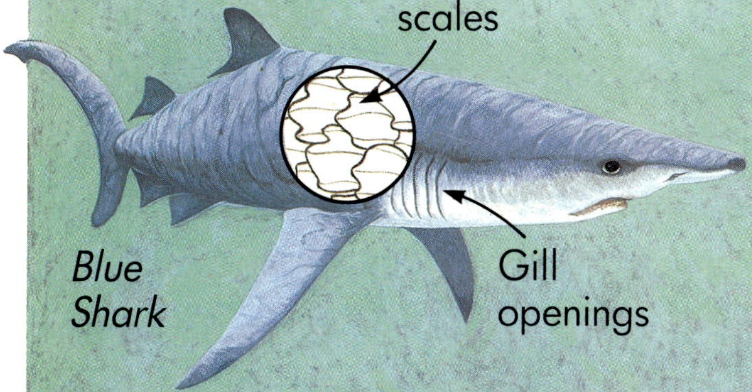

scales

Skate (a type of ray)

These openings lead to the gills.

Blue Shark

Gill openings

scales

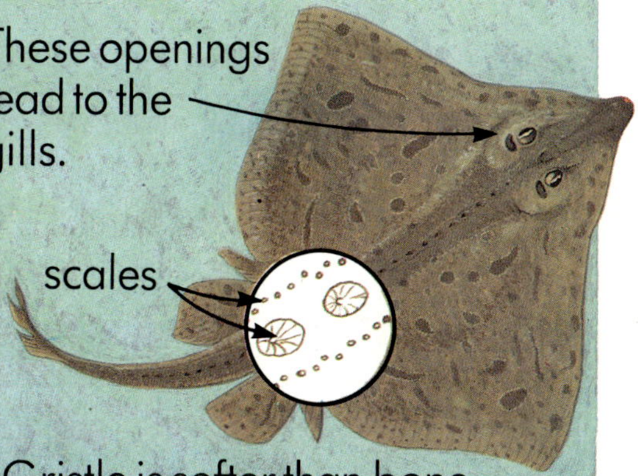

Sharks and rays have a skeleton made of gristle. Gristle is softer than bone, and can bend a little, but is still very tough. Sharks and rays are covered with lots of tiny scales. The scales are half buried in the skin.

3. Lampreys

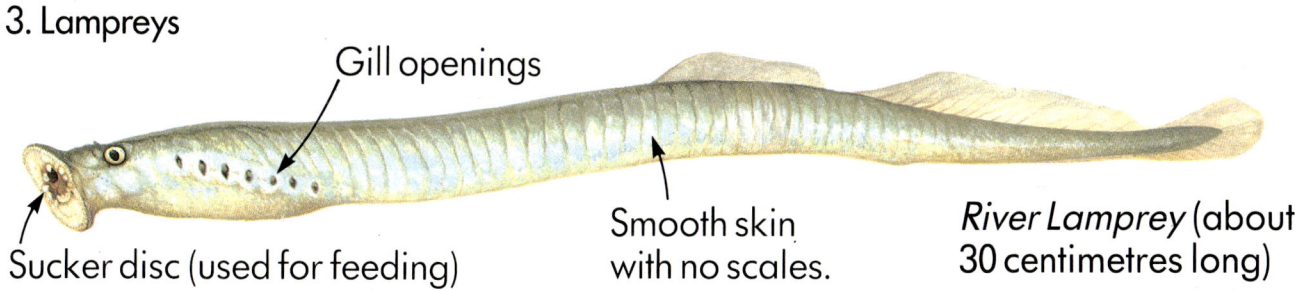

Gill openings

Sucker disc (used for feeding)

Smooth skin with no scales.

River Lamprey (about 30 centimetres long)

Lampreys have no jaws and no scales. The skeleton is made of gristle.

51

How fishes move

Most fishes swim using their fins. Some fins move the body forward. Others help to keep the fish the right way up.

The Bass's tail sweeps from side to side. This pushes the fish forward. The other fins keep the body steady.

The Manta Ray has huge side fins. They beat up and down like wings. The fish "flies" through the water.

The back fin of the Seahorse keeps moving in an S-shape. It drives the fish forwards.

The Eel's whole body wriggles to push the fish forward.

Eels usually have small fins.

Some fishes move in unusual ways.

*South American freshwater
Hatchet Fish*

Long
side
fin

Flying Fishes are chased
by dolphins and sharks.

Long
side
fins

Some Hatchet Fishes can leap from the water. They fly through the air by beating their fins very fast. As they do this, the fins make a buzzing sound.

Flying Fishes swim very fast under the water using the tail fin. Suddenly they burst through the surface and spread out their fins. They glide in the air.

long fins

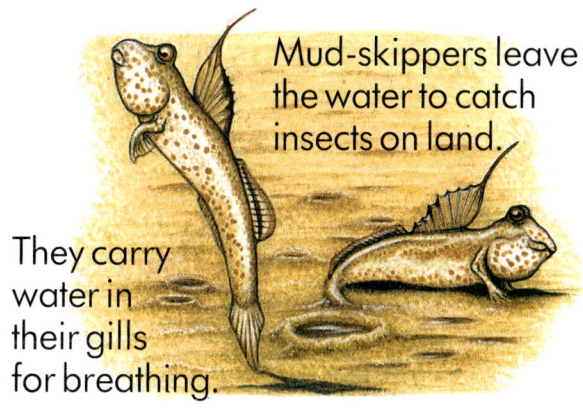

Mud-skippers leave the water to catch insects on land.

They carry water in their gills for breathing.

Frogfishes have fins at the ends of four short "arms". They crawl about amongst coral and seaweed looking for food.

Mud-skippers can jump. They curl the tail around against the mud. Suddenly they jerk the body straight. The whole fish jumps forwards.

How fishes breathe

Fishes need a gas called oxygen to live. There is oxygen in the water, and most fishes get it by using their gills. The blood inside the gills takes up oxygen from the water.

gill cover

Trout

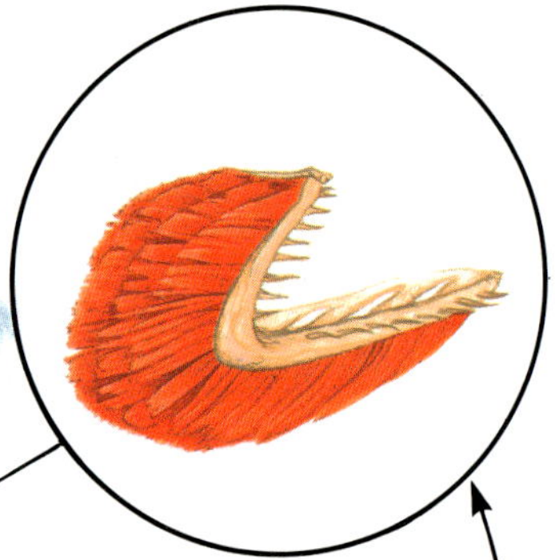

The gills look like this when the gill cover is taken away. They are bright red because they contain a lot of blood.

The pictures below show how most fishes breathe.

Mouth open
WATER

1. The fish gulps a big mouthful of water. Then it closes its mouth.

Mouth shut

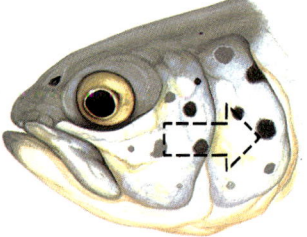

2. This pushes the water between the gills. The blood in the gills takes up the oxygen.

Mouth shut

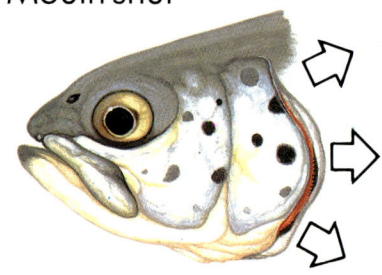

3. The blood carries oxygen around the body. The water comes out through the gill opening.

54

mouth

gill slits

Water enters through holes.

eyes

Underside of Thornback Ray.

Thornback Ray resting on the sand.

The mouth of a ray is on the underside of its body. When the ray rests on the sand, it cannot gulp a mouthful of clean water. Instead, it takes in water through two holes on top of its head. The water goes down over the gills and is pumped out through the gill slits.

Lungfishes have lungs as well as gills.

African Lungfishes usually live underwater in lakes. They use their gills and lungs to breathe. They gulp air at the surface of the water.

In hot weather, the lakes dry up. The Lungfish buries itself in the mud. It uses its lungs to breathe air through a hole.

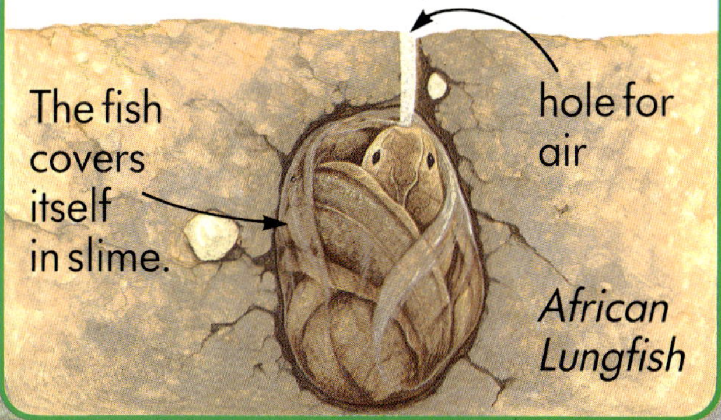

The fish covers itself in slime.

hole for air

African Lungfish

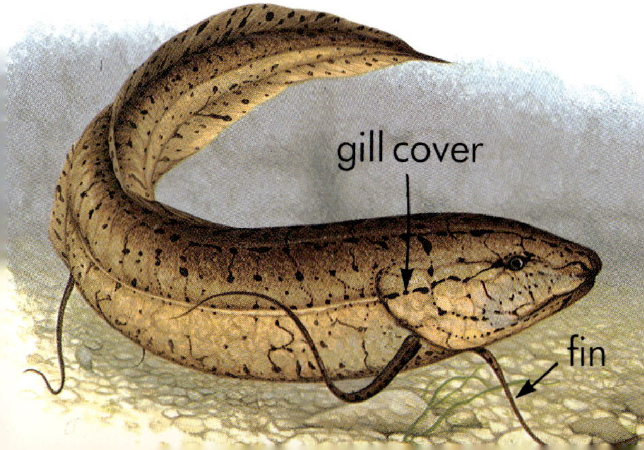

gill cover

fin

55

How fishes find their way around

Like us, fishes can smell, see, taste, and hear. They also have special senses to help them find their way around.

Smelling

Most fishes have two pairs of nostrils.

Moray Eel

A fish has a good sense of smell. It uses its nostrils for smelling, but not for breathing.

Seeing

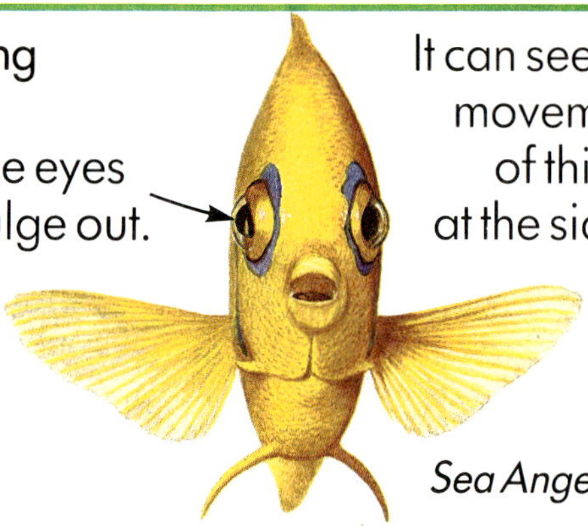

The eyes bulge out.

It can see the movement of things at the sides.

Sea Angelfish

Fishes can see very clearly in front of them, but not so clearly at the sides. Many fishes see in colour.

Tasting and feeling

Catfish

Some fishes have feelers on their chin and lips. The feelers are called barbels. The fish can taste with its barbels. It can also use them to search for food.

barbel

Hearing

Striped Drum Fish

Lateral line

Carp

Fishes have ears inside their heads. This fish lives in murky water, so hearing is more important to it than seeing. It finds other Drum Fish by making loud drumming noises.

Most fishes have a line running along each side of their body. It is called the lateral line. The little holes in the line can sense the movements made by other animals in the water.

A few fishes have a special part of the body which makes electricity.

This Elephant Fish can electrify the water around it.

These lines show where the fish sends electricity.

As Elephant Fishes move around, they notice anything which alters this electricity. This stops them from bumping into things. It also helps them to find each other. They can easily swim backwards using this sense.

Ways of catching food

Fishes do not have regular meals. They eat what they can when they can. Some may go without food for days. Others catch food all the time. The shape of a fish's mouth often shows how it catches its food.

Black Swallower

Food in the huge stomach.

Some deep sea fishes can open their mouths extra wide. They can swallow very large fishes. Their stomachs stretch to hold a big meal.

Basking Shark

gill rakers

This shark swims with its mouth wide open. Its throat is lined with curved pieces of gristle called gill rakers. These catch tiny animals.

Great White Shark

The Great White Shark is big and strong. It can catch almost anything in the sea. Its teeth are sharp and triangular. As each tooth wears away or falls out, a new tooth from the row behind it takes its place.

Some fishes catch their food in cunning ways.

African freshwater Butterfly Fish

This fish lies in wait just under the surface of the water. When an insect lands, the fish leaps to grab it.

Malaysian Archer Fish

When the insect falls into the water, the fish eats it.

This fish can spit water at insects and spiders above the surface. The tiny jet of water knocks them off plants.

Angler Fish

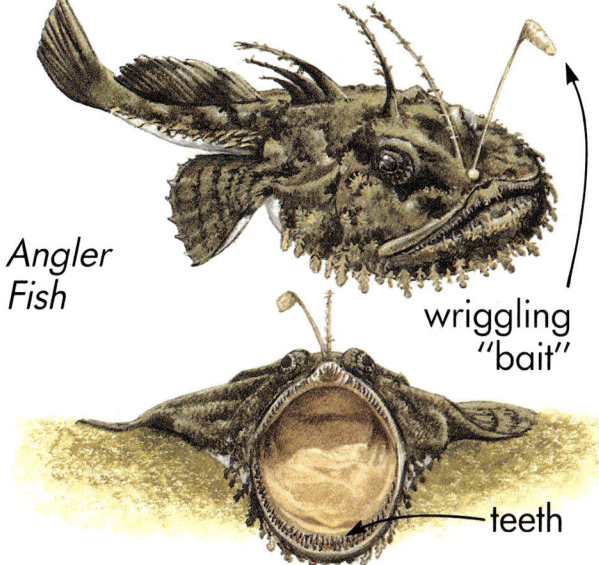

wriggling "bait"

teeth

Part of this fish's body forms a kind of "fishing rod" and "bait". Small fishes mistake the "bait" for food and come too close. They get caught and eaten.

American Garpike

hundreds of sharp teeth

The Garpike lies quietly at the surface or in the weeds. When a fish comes near, it turns slowly to face its prey, then charges.

59

Colours in fishes

Many fishes are covered with brightly coloured patterns. In their natural surroundings, these markings help them to hide.

The Mackerel's colouring helps it to avoid its enemies, such as birds and big fishes. It is well camouflaged.

It has a dark blue pattern on its back.

Its belly and sides are white.

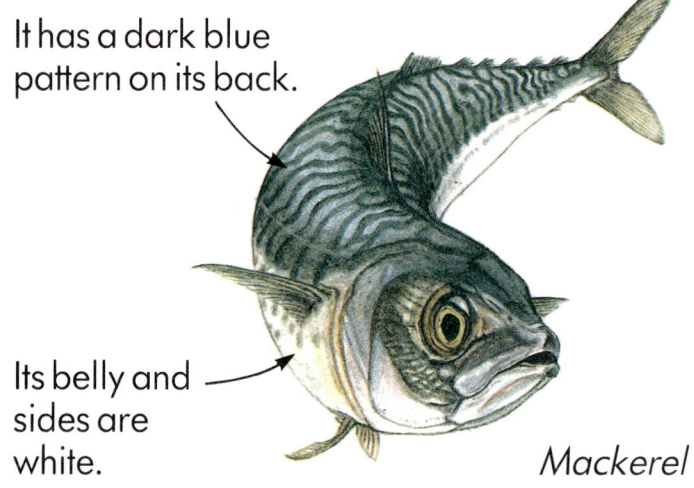

Mackerel

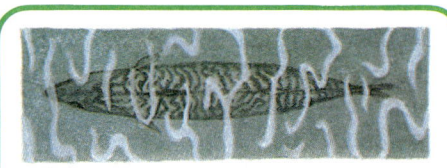

If you look down on a Mackerel from a boat, its blue back seems to merge with the water.

If you look up at a Mackerel from below, its white belly seems to merge with the sky.

Fishes like this Pike feed on other fishes. It lies in wait amongst the reeds. The blotches on its body blend with the reed stems, making it hard to see.

Many fishes living on the sea bed can change colour as they move about. The colour of this Australian Wobbegong (a shark) matches the sand and gravel.

Some fishes use bright colours or bold markings to trick their enemies or to warn them to keep away.

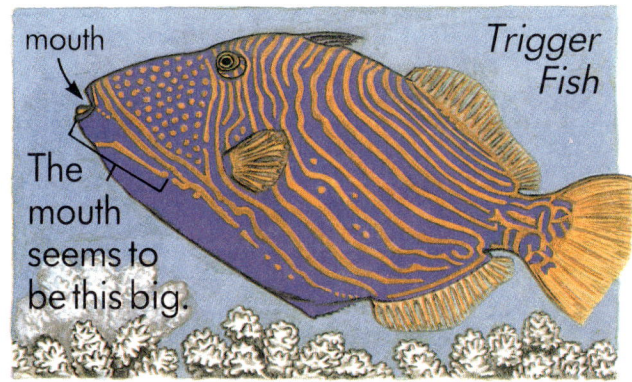

mouth

The mouth seems to be this big.

Trigger Fish

dark spot

tail

Long-nosed Butterfly Fish

eye

mouth

This Trigger Fish has dark markings on the lips and face. The mouth looks much bigger and fiercer than it really is. Other fishes keep away.

Many Butterfly Fishes have a dark spot near the tail. It looks like an eye. This confuses other fishes because the head seems to be where the tail is.

This fish has spines on its back and is brightly coloured. The spines have poison in them and the colours warn other fishes to keep away.

Red Fire Fish

Finding a mate and making a nest

Most fishes just come together in groups to lay their eggs. In some fishes, however, one male and one female form a pair. The male shows off to the female. This is called displaying.

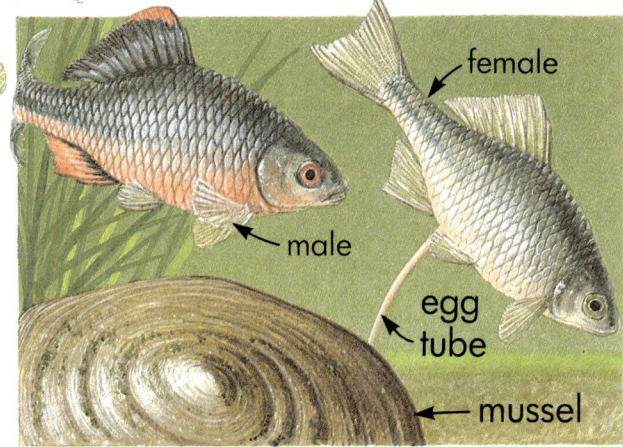

The male Stickleback displays his red belly to the female. This coaxes her to lay her eggs in the nest he has built. He drives other males away.

The male Bitterling displays to the female and leads her to a live mussel. She lays her eggs inside it through a special egg-laying tube.

The male Dragonet is brilliantly coloured. He has a very big pointed fin on his back. He keeps lifting it to attract a female.

Some fishes make a nest. Others just hide their eggs. But in both cases, the eggs are safe from being eaten or being washed away by the water.

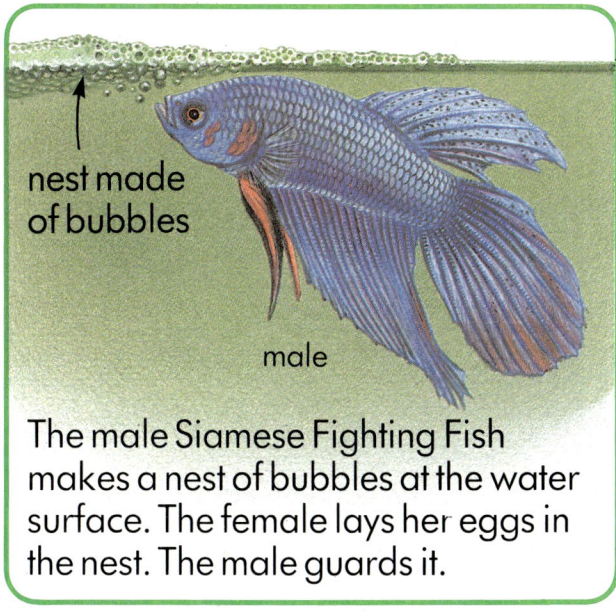

nest made of bubbles

male

The male Siamese Fighting Fish makes a nest of bubbles at the water surface. The female lays her eggs in the nest. The male guards it.

hook for fighting

male

female

eggs

The female Salmon scrapes a nest in the river gravel. The nest is called a redd. Males fight each other to win a female and her redd.

Californian Grunion

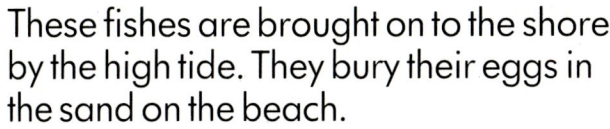

These fishes are brought on to the shore by the high tide. They bury their eggs in the sand on the beach.

African Lyretail

male

female

eggs

Lyretails live in small pools which often dry up. They bury their eggs in the mud. The baby fishes do not hatch until it rains again.

Fish eggs and babies

Most fishes lay lots of very small eggs. Some eggs float in the sea, and others stick to plants and rocks. The parents do not usually look after them.

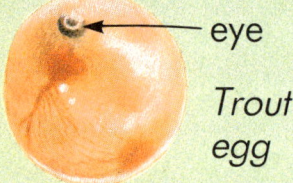

eye

Trout egg

Fins beginning to grow.

yolk

newly-hatched Trout

1. Fish eggs have a lot of yolk inside them. The baby grows by feeding on the yolk.

2. The baby fish has hatched, but it still lives on the stored food in the yolk.

young Trout

Remains of yolk.

3. The yolk lasts until the fins of the young fish are fully grown.

Some fishes lay a few large eggs. Dogfish eggs are laid inside a case which becomes hard in the sea. The case protects the egg as it grows.

Dogfish

Egg case of Dogfish

Some bony fishes look after their eggs until the young hatch out.

Baby Guppy being born.

The female Guppy keeps her eggs inside her body. The young hatch just before they are born.

babies

pouch

Male Seahorses carry the female's eggs in a pouch until they hatch.

eggs

Male Tilapias carry the eggs in their mouth. They also shelter the young fishes in their mouth.

Spurdog Shark

female

pup

Some sharks give birth to babies, called pups. Others lay eggs in a hard egg case and leave them to hatch out.

Life in fresh water

Many different kinds of fishes can live in the same river, because they like different parts of the river.

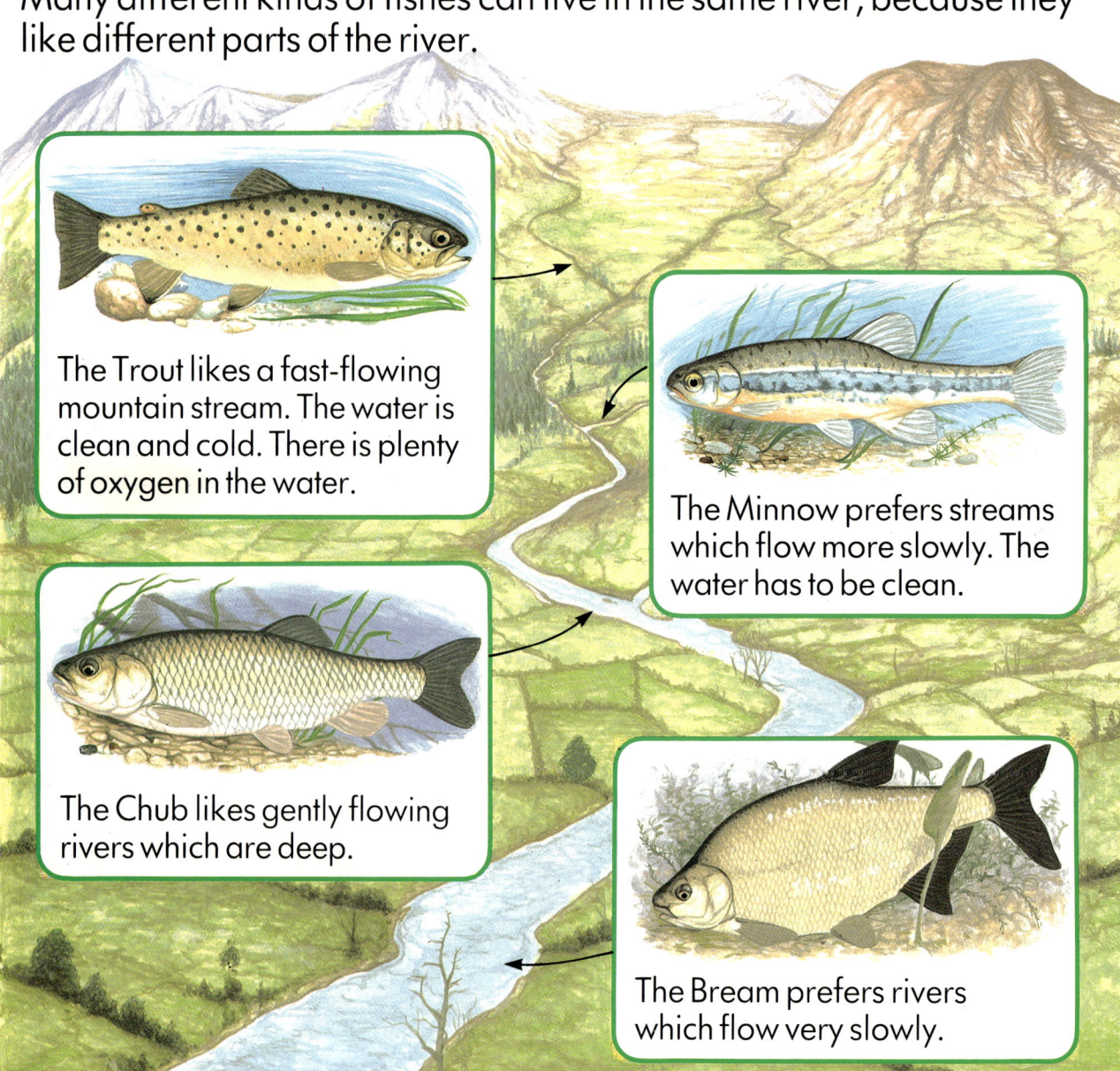

The Trout likes a fast-flowing mountain stream. The water is clean and cold. There is plenty of oxygen in the water.

The Chub likes gently flowing rivers which are deep.

The Minnow prefers streams which flow more slowly. The water has to be clean.

The Bream prefers rivers which flow very slowly.

The water in some streams and rivers flows very fast. The fishes must make sure that they are not swept away by the strong current.

Asian hillstream Loach

water current

Some fishes, like this baby Salmon, hide behind stones to escape the current.

This fish is flat underneath. It can cling to big stones on the bed of the stream.

These fishes are well suited to the places where they live.

South American freshwater Angelfish

Blind Tetra

This Angelfish is very thin. It can swim between plant stems, and hide in them from its enemies.

This fish lives in freshwater lakes in caves. It has no eyes, but it can find its way around in the dark.

Life in the shallow seas

The shallow seas around the seashore have lots of food and hiding places for fishes. Many different kinds of fishes live there.

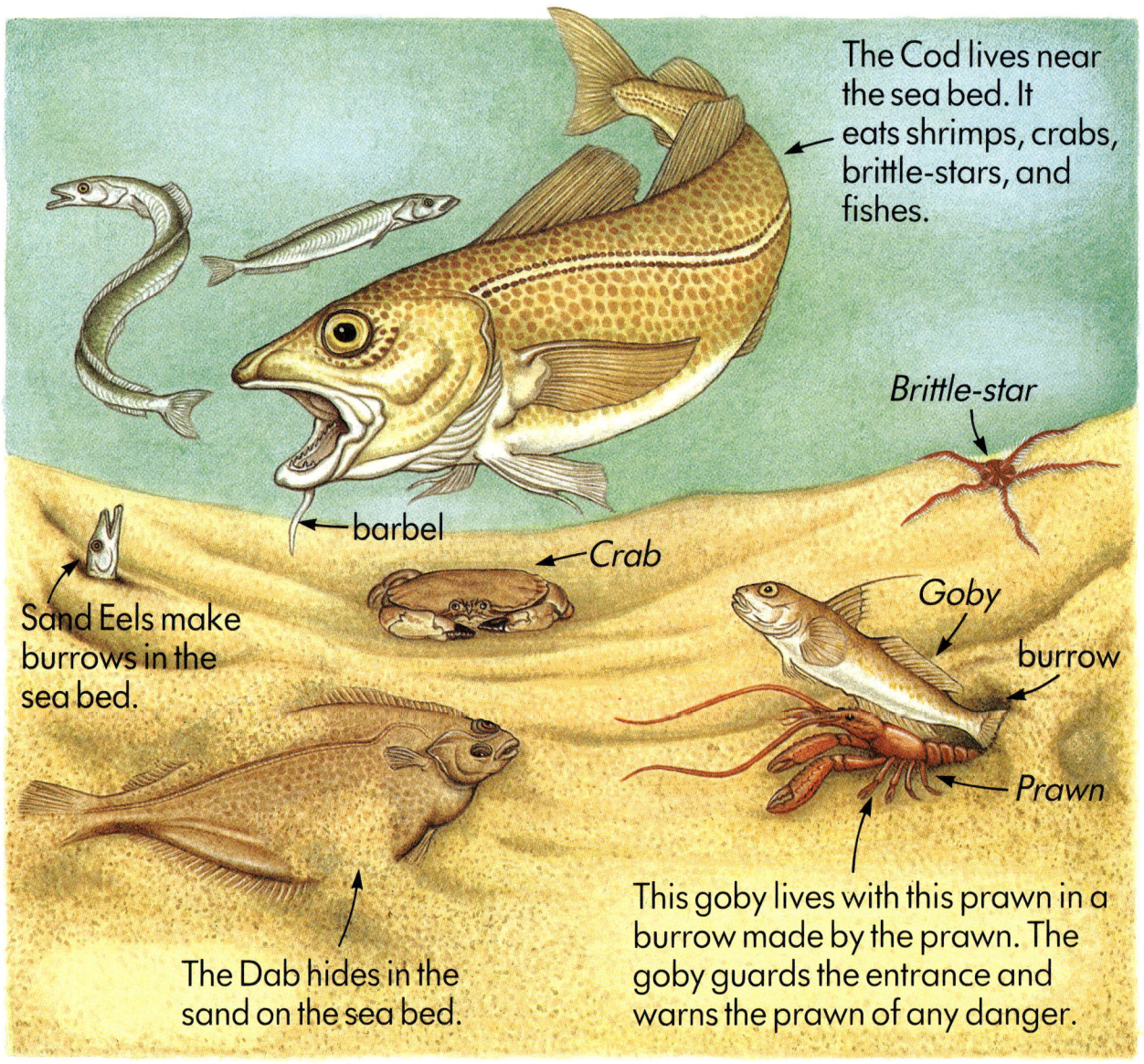

The Cod lives near the sea bed. It eats shrimps, crabs, brittle-stars, and fishes.

Brittle-star

barbel

Crab

Sand Eels make burrows in the sea bed.

Goby

burrow

Prawn

The Dab hides in the sand on the sea bed.

This goby lives with this prawn in a burrow made by the prawn. The goby guards the entrance and warns the prawn of any danger.

A coral reef is the best place to find fishes. They can live or hide all over the reef. Some fishes eat coral, as well as sheltering in it.

Surgeon Fishes feed on small plants that grow on the coral.

Schools of Damsel Fishes live close to the reef.

Parrot Fishes have big teeth. They crunch up the coral.

The anemone clings to the coral.

This sea anemone lets only this kind of Clown Fish live between its tentacles. Other kinds of fish get stung. The Clown Fish gets shelter, and brings the anemone food.

Butterfly Fishes have many tiny teeth. They nibble food from cracks in the coral.

Life in the deep seas

The deep sea is a bleak place to live. It is dark and very cold. No plants and not many animals live there. The fishes have to make sure they catch whatever food is around.

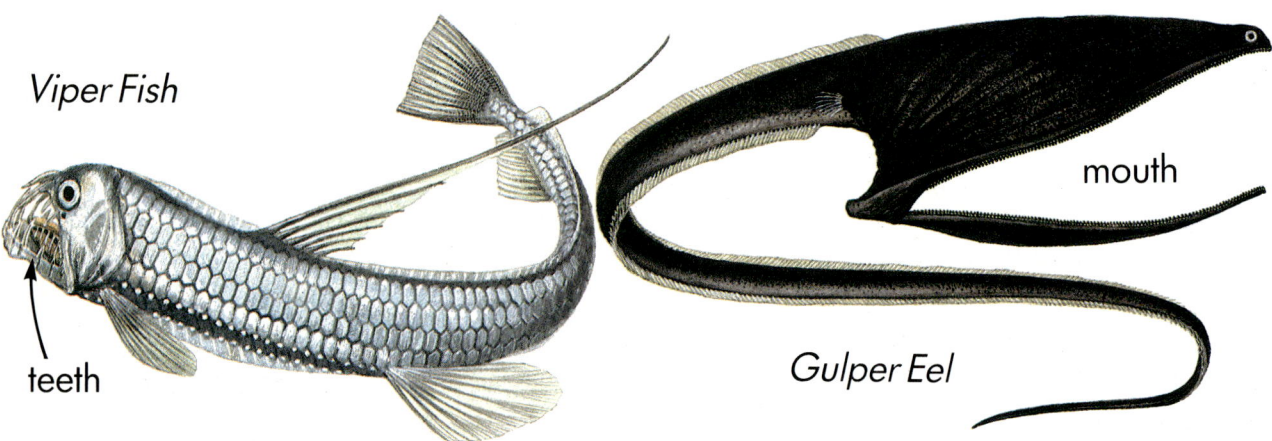

Viper Fish

teeth

Gulper Eel

mouth

Some fishes, like this Viper Fish, catch their prey with their big teeth.

Others have a mouth that is very big for the size of their body.

Many fishes eat small animals which live on the ocean floor.

Tripod Fish

long fins

Spiny-eel

Rat-tail

The Tripod Fish props itself up on its long fins. The long rays in these fins can sense food buried in the mud.

These two fishes swim with their heads down to find brittle-stars and small shrimps that hide in the sea bed.

Most deep sea fishes are black in colour. Some of them have special parts of their bodies that make light. When these lights are turned off, the fishes disappear into the darkness of the deep sea.

Snipe-eel

This fish has large eyes, so it can see quite well in the dark. It has no lights. It feeds on tiny shrimp-like animals.

Schools of Lantern Fishes keep together by flashing their lights on and off.

The Dragon Fish has a red light and a green light near each eye. It uses the lights like a torch to find food.

This deep sea Angler Fish has lights on its "fishing rods". It grabs other fishes that are attracted to the lights.

INDEX